WHITE CRANE

WHITE CRANE

Love Songs of the Sixth Dalai Lama

Translated by
Geoffrey R. Waters

Companions for the Journey Series: Volume 14

WHITE PINE PRESS / BUFFALO, NEW YORK

Publication of this book was made possible, in part, with public funds
from the New York State Council on the Arts, a State Agency.

Printed and bound in the United States of America.

First Edition

Library of Congress Control Number: 2007921246

ISBN-13: 978-1-893996-82-3
ISBN-10: 1-893996-82-4

Published by
White Pine Press
P.O. Box 236
Buffalo, New York 14201

www.whitepine.org

For the People of Tibet

The Norwegian Nobel Committee, awarding the 1989 Nobel Peace Prize to the Fourteenth Dalai Lama:

> "It would be difficult to cite any historical example of a minority's struggle to secure its rights, in which a more conciliatory attitude to the adversary has been adopted than in the case of the Dalai Lama."

The Fourteenth Dalai Lama, accepting the 1989 Nobel Peace Prize in Oslo, Norway, December 12, 1989:

> "In conclusion, let me share with you a short prayer which gives me great inspiration and determination:
>
> > For as long as space endures,
> > And for as long as living beings remain,
> > Until then may I, too, abide
> > To dispel the misery of the world."
> >
> > (Śāntideva, *Bodhicaryāvatāra* 10:55)

Contents

Translator's Preface

This little book had a gestation period of almost thirty-five years. In 1971, when I began my graduate studies in Chinese and Tibetan at Indiana University, I became intrigued by references in Tibetan histories to Tsangyang Gyatso, the Sixth Dalai Lama: supposedly a libertine poet among a lineage of reincarnated lamas.

After surviving a year of Friedrich Bischoff's early morning intensive Tibetan reading course, I decided to try translating the Sixth Dalai Lama's poems. I found four different editions of the text in the Tibetan collection of the Indiana University library, collated them, and went to work on an initial translation of the poems, numbering sixty-six. Once they were finished, I presented them in Willis Barnstone's seminar on poetry translation. Prof. Barnstone encouraged me to submit them to the Asia Society's Asian Literature Program, which had also been able to arrange publication for some of my translations of the Tang woman poet Yu Xuanji.

In 1974, I received a small grant from the Asia Society to support final preparation of the poems for publication. In the course of discussions of the project with a fellow student in the Tibetan program, Gary Houston, we decided to make a collaborative effort at revising my earlier translations.

At Houston's urging, we also solicited the help of Professor Helmut Hoffmann, then teaching at Indiana. Hoffman—a specialist in Tibetan tantricism—felt quite strongly that a powerful Tantric magician lay behind the persona and works of the libertine poet. He believed the poems were larded with allusions to esoteric rituals. He began preparing a long scholarly introduction for the book along those lines.

As sometime happens, our three-way collaboration soon ended prematurely. We disagreed mainly on the aesthetics of the translator's voice, but also on the relevance of Hoffman's heavy Tantric material to a thin book of folksongs intended for the popular market. We parted friends and fate carried us off in different directions. Later, our Ph.D.s in hand, Houston became a Methodist minister and I became a banker, eventually living and working eleven years in Hong Kong. In 1982, Houston and Hoffman had the results of their continued collaboration published in India.

My wife and I spent some time on vacation in central Tibet during the summer of 1987. In the course of exploring the old Tibetan quarter of Lhasa, we found a tiny bookstore. On a whim, I went in to look for a Tibetan language street map, and to see what Tibetan books might be available. The clerk did not speak Mandarin, so in my best schoolboy Tibetan, I asked her if she had any books about Tsangyang Gyatso. She smiled broadly and showed me two books: both were recent typeset editions of the so-called *Secret Biography of the Sixth Dalai Lama,* but one also included a much larger set of poems attributed to him. For a few dollars, I bought a map and two copies of each book. We used the map to continue exploring the old town. The books, I put away for that rainy day when I would dig out my 1974 manuscript and revise it for publication.

Years passed, and those rainy days came from time to time. This book is the result.

I would like to acknowledge my former collaborators, the Rev. Gary W. Houston of Bloomington, Indiana, and the late Helmut Hoffmann; and the help of Professor (now Emeritus) Thubten Jigme Norbu, also of Indiana University, who was indulgent and generous with his time and insights into a few perplexing colloquialisms; Willis Barnstone; Zelda Bradburd, formerly of the Asia Society; and, as always, Friedrich A. Bischoff, who in addition to teaching me a few things about Chinese over the years, managed to teach me literary Tibetan as well. All the errors, of course, are mine.

—Geoff Waters
Glendale, California
November 2006

INTRODUCTION

Tsangyang Gyatso was the Sixth Dalai Lama. The present Dalai Lama, Tenzin Gyatso, is the Fourteenth. Tibetans believe all the Dalai Lamas have been reincarnations of the bodhisattva Avalokiteśvara—Chenresi in Tibetan, the Buddhist deity who is Tibet's special protector. As people have their various moods and facets, the gods have theirs. Tibetans love the memory of the unlikely Sixth: a libertine and poet from a line of god-kings, whose name means "Ocean of Pure Melody." Tibet is a land of contradictions. If Chenresi wishes to show an earthier side from time to time, are we to disapprove?

Tsangyang Gyatso was born in 1683 and died near the end of 1706. He was a pawn in a political game which began five hundred years before his birth, and which continues today.

One of the earliest moves in that game was in 1207, when Tibetan representatives surrendered to Chinggis Khan's advancing Mongol army. By becoming early vassals of the Khan they avoided the grisly fate of many other nations in the Mongols' path.

In 1244, Chinggis' grandson, Godan Khan appointed the head of the Sakya sect of Tibetan Buddhism to be Regent of Tibet. Later, the political supremacy of the Sakya sect was reinforced when its head became the religious teacher of Qubilai Khan, Godan's successor. In 1270, the Mongols confirmed the head of the Sakya sect's complete political and religious authority over Tibet.

Over the following decades, Tibetan religious teachers came to exert great personal influence over the Mongol leaders. Although the Mongols may technically have made the Tibetans their vassals, in the centuries that followed, the Tibetans utterly defeated the Mongols with an army of monks. They did it by gradually converting the Mongols into devout Buddhists, softening their warlike spirit.

The Mongols went on to conquer China in the late thirteenth century and became mired in the bureaucratic quicksand of the Chinese Empire. By 1368, when the Mongol dynasty was overthrown in China, their influence in Tibet had waned. Along with it waned the political power of the Sakya regents.

In 1578, Altan Khan, leader of the Tümed clan of the Mongols, honored his tutor, the third patriarch of the Gelukpa sect of Tibetan Buddhism, with the title Dalai Lama, "Ocean of Wisdom." Altan Khan also posthumously conferred the title on the two earlier patriarchs of the sect, making the Dalai Lama who first bore the title actually the Third Dalai Lama, Sönam Gyatso (1543-1588). The Gelukpa patriarchs were believed to be incarnations of Chenresi. For that reason, the title was passed to succeeding reincarnations: boys born shortly after the death of the incumbent, who were discovered as small children, raised as monks and eventually succeeded to the office.

When Sönam Gyatso died in Mongolia, his successor was discovered there, a great-grandson of Altan Khan, who became the Fourth Dalai Lama, Yönden Gyatso (1589-1616). Chenresi seems not to have been above a bit of political expediency.

Mongol-Tibetan involvement increased again from this period. When Tibet was politically united under the Fifth Dalai Lama (1617-1682), Ngawang Losang Gyatso, it was with the significant support of Gushri Khan of the Qošot clan, Mongol rivals of the Tümed. The enduring political and religious primacy of the Dalai Lama was first established by the strong steps taken by the Fifth to unify the country under the tutelage of the Gelukpa order.

In 1644, the Manchu people invaded China from the

northeast, conquered it, and established their Qing Dynasty. The Fifth Dalai Lama made an early state visit to the Manchu court in Peking. One aim of his journey was to play off the Manchus against the Mongols, thus hoping to neutralize them both. From then until his death, the nation-building Fifth Dalai Lama ruled Tibet almost as an absolute monarch.

THE SIXTH DALAI LAMA

When the Fifth Dalai Lama died in 1682, his Regent, Sanggye Gyatso, did not reveal the Dalai Lama's death in the usual way. Instead, he announced that the Dalai Lama had gone into seclusion for a long period of meditation. The regent feared the Mongols or Manchus might use the interregnum as an opportunity or pretext for renewing their interference in Tibet. He felt it crucial to conceal the death of the Fifth until he could discover, raise, and train the new reincarnation in seclusion until the Sixth was old enough to assume the throne as an adult. By doing this, the Regent hoped to thwart Mongol and Manchu ambitions in Tibet and ensure Tibet's continued strong self-rule.

His plan might have worked had not Chenresi chosen that moment to present such an unexpected aspect. Almost any other successor might have been able to carry off the succession, but the Sixth Dalai Lama was to be nothing like the Fifth.

The Regent maintained order for thirteen years, until the

secret of the Fifth Dalai Lama's death became known. Tsangyang Gyatso was ordained and enthroned in a rush. He had led a sheltered, pampered, secular life. Because of the need to keep his existence a secret, Tsangyang Gyatso entered religious training almost ten years later than most of his predecessors or successors. By that age, his temperament and personality had been formed outside the monastic tradition. Despite his belated ordination, he grew up more a wastrel than a monk, more a minstrel than a king. He loved women and drinking. He cared little for his ceremonial duties, preferring to build gardens and sing songs. It is said of him that he rarely slept alone or retired much before dawn.

His Fate

Earlier, to balance the influence of the Qošot clan, who had helped him into power, the Fifth Dalai Lama had opened contacts with yet another rival Mongol clan, the Dzungars. The Regent maintained these contacts after the death of the Fifth. He feared Lhabzang Khan, the ambitious new leader of the Qošots, would try to reassert his clan's old prerogatives in Tibetan affairs.

The regent's moves were to no avail. In 1705, Lhabzang allied with the Manchus and invaded Lhasa. Lhabzang's pretext was to remove the licentious Sixth Dalai Lama and his evil Regent from power. His real aim was to reduce the roles both of the Regent and the Dzungars, with whom both the Qošots and Manchus had been at odds.

The Regent was killed, and the young Dalai Lama removed from Lhasa by force. In late 1706, the Manchus denounced Tsangyang Gyatso as an impostor and took him off to exile in China. They installed in his place a young man named Ngawang Yeshe Gyatso, whom they had groomed as a replacement. Ngawang Yeshe Gyatso was not recognized as the Sixth Dalai Lama by the Tibetan people, but with Lhabzang's troops in Lhasa to prop him up, he held the office until 1717.

Tsangyang Gyatso never reached his Chinese exile alive. A report of his death en route, allegedly from an illness, reached the Manchu Emperor in Peking in December 1706:

> On this date the Court of Colonial Affairs submitted a proposal to the Emperor as follows: "The Lama Shangnan Duoerji, detached at Xining, reports: 'Lhasa dispatched the false Dalai Lama to you, but being brought as far as the vicinity of Xining, he has now died of a disease.' Because the false Dalai Lama's conduct was rebellious, and because he has now died en route, we recommend an Imperial order be issued to Shangnan Duoerji to have the corpse discarded." The Emperor approved the request. (*The True Records of the Emperor Kangxi.* December 4, 1706]

The life of the historical Sixth Dalai Lama probably ended there. But, according to the so-called *Secret Biography of the Sixth Dalai Lama*, he escaped his Chinese captors by using magic and spent some years in secret pilgrimages to the holy places of Buddhism in India, Nepal, Tibet and China. Later, the hero of the *Secret Biography* settled in Mongolia until his death in 1746. In another version, he escaped, but went on to China and spent the rest of his long life meditating in a cave on Mt. Wutai in Shanxi.

THE AFTERMATH

Soon after the death of the Sixth, Chenresi was reborn as the Seventh Dalai Lama, Kalsang Gyatso, at Litang, a town in a remote part of eastern Tibet. One of Tsangyang Gyatso's poems foresaw this rebirth:

> You, bird, white crane,
> Lend me the power of your wings!
> I won't fly far:
> Just to Litang, then home again.

In 1717, the Dzungars drove their rival Qošots out of Lhasa and dethroned the replacement Dalai Lama, Ngawang Yeshe Gyatso. Soon, they suffered the same fate at the hands of the Manchus. Once and for all, the Manchus replaced the Mongols as patrons of the Gelukpa and stationed a pair of political observers in Lhasa.

The Manchus exercised this nominal jurisdiction over Tibet until they were overthrown in the Chinese Revolution of 1912. After they were overthrown, Tibet repudiated the former Manchu claims to sovereignty. Unfortunately, the new twentieth century found Tibet at a geopolitical crossroads between the interests of the Russians, the Chinese, and the British in India.

The new Republican Chinese government of 1912 and their successors until the present day found it convenient to portray themselves as inheritors of the Mongol and Manchu mantle in Tibet to legitimize their occupation. In doing so, however, they have invested that mantle retroactively with a degree of concrete authority and physical control it rarely enjoyed in reality. This, to Tibet's sorrow.

China's attempts to rationalize its invasion, subjugation, and destruction of Tibet during the period from 1951 onwards have this tragic link with the unwilling pawn who died on the road to China 250 years before.

Tibetans prefer to remember the romantic and the poet rather than the hapless political pawn or the unlikely religious ruler. In their book, *A Cultural History of Tibet,* Snellgrove and Richardson relate:

> Many Tibetans can still recall the traditional
> account of his appearance—in the blue silk
> robe of a lay nobleman, wearing his hair in
> long black locks, bedecked with rings and

jewelry, and carrying a bow and quiver. His lyrics have retained a universal popularity throughout the country; and as a poet of a most unusual kind for Tibet... [he] deserves a place in any cultural history. (pp. 205-6)

The Poems

This book includes 120 poems. The first sixty-six, the ones I translated in 1972, are the core set traditionally attributed to Tsangyang Gyatso.

The 1981 Beijing edition, one of the books I bought in Lhasa in 1987, contained the core set plus almost sixty additional poems selected from a large manuscript in the Tibetan collection of the Central Academy of National Minorities in Beijing entitled *Rig 'dzin tsang dbyangs rgya mtsho'i gsung mgur* [The Poems of Rigdzin Tsangyang Gyatso]. From that edition, I added an additional thirty-eight poems.

The remaining sixteen were drawn from a complete transliteration of the same large manuscript, over 450 poems in total, presented as an Appendix to Per Sørenson's meticulous 1990 edition of the core poems.

The Sixth Dalai Lama's poems are like small windows through which one glimpses the life he led. Most of them are made up of four unrhymed lines of six syllables each, yielding something between the Japanese haiku and the Chinese *jueju* (quatrain) in their brevity.

Themes vary. Love lyrics predominate: laments for lost or unrequited affection, bits of advice to lovers from folk wisdom, and descriptions of his lovers in terms both flattering and biting. A number of religious verses are found as well, as one might expect from a people whose religion has so deeply penetrated every facet of their daily lives. Their essence is simplicity and directness. They dismiss the weighty or philosophical themes of "serious" poetry, being instead simply jingles or folk songs meant to please the ear and recall a smile.

It is also possible, as some scholars have tried, to read into these poems detailed allusions to the political intrigues of the day, including the conflict of wills between the Sixth Dalai Lama and his Regent. Per Sørenson has explained these allusions in his 1990 study, so for our purposes, we will leave them aside.

Since these poems have been preserved mainly in the oral tradition, questions of textual provenance and even authorship are not particularly crucial. Many of our usual tools for establishing the originality and genuineness of literary texts are of little use. These poems have come down to us associated with Tsangyang Gyatso's name in the oral, folklore tradition of Tibet. We ought to do as the Tibetans have done for four centuries: simply enjoy them as they are.

The Love Songs of the Sixth Dalai Lama

1. From the peaks of the eastern mountains
   A bright white moon has risen,
   And a young girl's face
   Shines round in my mind.

2. Young shoots planted last year
   Are this year's sheaves of straw.
   Young men age, their bodies grow
   More crooked than a southern bow.

3. If the one who's caught my fancy
   Would stay with me forever,
   It would be like finding
   A jewel from the bottom of the sea.

4.   I met her on the way by chance,
       A girl with a fragrant body;
       Like finding a small white turquoise,
       Then tossing it away.

5.   I look at the beautiful face
       Of a nobleman's daughter:
       High in a tree, a peach
       Ripening out of reach.

6.   I think about her all the time;
       At night my sleep is ruined.
       By day, she eludes me,
       And leaves me worn with care.

7.   The season of flowers is finished,
   But the turquoise bee is not sad;
   Our love's delights have ended,
   Neither have I any reason for sadness.

8.   Hoarfrost on the blades of grass,
   Harbinger of the cold winter wind,
   The winter wind that breaks the bond
   Between the flowers and the bee.

9.   Though the goose loved the marsh,
   And wanted to linger.
   Ice covered the lake,
   And sadly he took wing.

10.   The ferryboat has no heart,
But the horse-head turns to look;
My heartless lover,
Left me without looking back.

11.   The market-girl and I
Were bound by a three-word oath.
Like the mottled snake uncoils upon the earth,
So our promise came undone.

12.   My childhood sweetheart's lucky flag
Is waving up in a willow tree.
Please brother, keeper of the willow grove,
Don't throw stones to bring it down!

13.   Written letters, black and small,
        If you get them wet, they're ruined;
        An unwritten image in your mind,
        You can't erase, no matter how you try.

14.   Once marked by the small black seal,
        The secrets sealed cannot be spoken.
        May the seal of discretion and modesty
        Be placed on both our hearts.

15.   O blooming mallow flower,
        If you go as an offering,
        Let this young turquoise bee
        Go into the temple with you!

16.   If the one I love,
             Leaves me for a life of faith,
             This young man won't stay behind:
             I'll go meditate in a mountain cave.

17.   I went before a learned lama
             To seek his spiritual teaching.
             But I couldn't keep my mind on it,
             And escaped to be with my lover.

18.   I try to imagine my lama's face;
             It ought to appear, but doesn't.
             I try not to imagine my lover's face;
             But clear and bright she shines in my mind.

19.   If a mind obsessed as I am with you
        Turned to holy religion,
        In one lifetime, in this very body,
        Buddhahood indeed!

20.   Melted snow from Crystal Mountain,
        Dew from a magic ginseng leaf,
        Yeast from the nectar of immortality,
        The barmaid is a goddess of wisdom.
        If we drink this beer with a vow of purity,
        We need never fear perdition!

21.   It's time to hang the prayer flags,
        We raise them waving in the wind;
        From the daughter of a good family,
        I get my wish, an invitation comes.

22. Their smiling face, their fair skin,
    I see her there, sitting among the girls.
    If you watch, you will see her wink
    When she steals a glance at me.

23. Fallen too much in love,
    I asked her, "Can we be as one?"
    She said, "Only death will divide us,
    Nothing will part us while still we live."

24. If I do as my lover wishes,
    My religious destiny will be lost;
    But, if I go meditate on some far mountain,
    Her heart will break.

25.   Like a bee caught in a web,
       The restless mind of this child from Gong;
       Three days he's been her bedmate,
       Wrestling with his life of religious duty.

26.   If the lover you have set your heart on
       Has immodest or shameful thoughts,
       Even if her turquoise pin could talk,
       You wouldn't know it.

27.   Smiling with her white teeth,
       She finally wins the young man's favor:
       "Please promise me," he asks,
       "These warm feeling come from your heart."

28.   I met my lover by chance,
        You, the barmaid, married us;
        If any bad karma results,
        I ask you to take care of it.

29.   If you don't confide in your parents,
        But tell your lover instead,
        Because your lover has so many admirers,
        Your rivals will hear all your secrets.

30.   My beloved is the goddess Manohara;
        Even though I, the hunter, caught her,
        The powerful ruler of men,
        Prince Sudhana has taken her away.

31. When you have a jewel,
     You don't appreciate its value.
     When you lose it to someone else,
     How your heart will ache!

32. The one I came to love
     Has been taken to marry another.
     Now my spirit is careworn,
     My body wasting away.

33. My lover has been stolen,
     I should cast lots and consult the stars.
     She was a faithful, passionate girl,
     Now I see her only in my dreams.

34.　　If this girl is immortal,
　　　　And the beer never runs out,
　　　　Then as my place of refuge,
　　　　Will I take this girl forever.

35.　　Was this girl not born of mother?
　　　　Is she a peach-tree's daughter?
　　　　Her fancy fades faster
　　　　Than peach blossoms wither.

36.　　Is my childhood sweetheart,
　　　　Descended from wolves?
　　　　If you give them a feast of flesh and skin,
　　　　They'll still run off to the hills again.

37.   Wild horses running in the hills
Can be caught with nets or ropes;
But, if your lover deserts you,
Even magic won't bring her back.

38.   As rocks and wind combine
To fray a vulture's feathers;
Her craftiness and deceit
Have worn me out.

39.   A yellow cloud with a black heart
Is the source of frost and hail;
That man, neither lay nor monk,
Is an enemy of Buddha's teaching.

40. A place with melted surface and ice below
    Is no place to lead a horse;
    By a new lover's side
    Is no place to tell your secrets.

41. I am like the full moon
    Of the mid-month night;
    The rabbit who lives in the full moon is also
    Finished when his short month is over.

42. Though the moon has waned,
    It will return next month.
    When the lucky white moon
    Is once more high, we'll meet again.

43.   Mt. Sumeru, center of the world,
Please remain fixed and steady;
I have no wish for the sun and moon
To turn in the wrong direction!

44.   O new slight moon of the third night,
You come out in your gown of white;
Just as you would if you were full again,
Please grant our wish tonight.

45.   Dweller in the Ten Realms of Perfection,
Oath-bound Adamantine Protector of the Faith,
If you have magic and power,
Drive away the enemies of the Teaching!

46.   When the cuckoo flew North from Mön,
He brought the sweet dew of a warmer season.
After my lover and I are together,
Body and soul rise languid and at ease.

47   If you don't think deeply in your hearts
About impermanence and death,
No matter how clever you think you are,
You will be like simpletons.

48.   That dog, whether tiger-dog or leopard-dog,
Can be tamed if you feed her;
But, this bad-tempered woman,
The closer we are, the worse her temper!

49.   Even though I have slept with soft bodies,
      I still don't know the depths of love;
      But, drawing a diagram on the ground,
      I can measure how the stars move.

50.   My lover and I have a rendezvous
      Deep in a beautiful southern forest;
      Except for a talking parrot,
      No one knows about us.
      "Please do us a favor, talking parrot,
      Don't let people know our secret!"

51.   Many people live in Lhasa,
      But the Chongjay people are the finest.
      The sweetheart that I desire
      Came here from Chongjay.

52.	Little beard, you old dog,
	You notice more than any man;
	Don't say I rose in the night,
	Don't say I returned at dawn.

53.	Last night I went to find my lover,
	This morning snow has fallen;
	Now my secret doesn't matter:
	My footprints follow me in the snow.

54.	When I dwell in the Potala,
	My name is "Sagacious Ocean of Melody;"
	When I linger down in Shö,
	They call me "Mighty King of Lovers."

55. With your soft flesh beneath the quilt,
    My faithful, passionate lover,
    Please don't say anything deceitful now,
    That would rob me of all this richness.

56. His hat is on his head.
    His braids fall down his back.
    "Go in peace," she says.
    "Stay in peace," he says.
    "I'll be so sad," she tells him.
    He says, "We'll meet again soon."

57. You, bird, white crane,
    Lend me the power of your wings!
    I won't fly far:
    Just to Litang, then home again.

58.   The King of Hell has a mirror
        Which reveals your karma clearly.
        In this life, my fate was undeserved.
        May his mirror reveal the truth when I am dead.

59.   The fortune-telling arrow hits the mark,
        Its head driving deep into the earth;
        To meet my dearest lover,
        I follow the footprints of my heart.

60.   Peacocks from the east of India,
        Parrots from the lowlands of Gong;
        Born in places far apart,
        They meet in Lhasa, "Wheel of the Law."

61.   Everything people said about me,
      True or not, it didn't hurt.
      With three small steps,
      I joined the charming barmaid instead.

62.   The willow loves the bird,
      The bird, the willow;
      If they continue to be friends,
      The fierce gray hawk won't get his way.

63.   In the short time we have left,
      I can only ask you this:
      "In our next life, children once more,
      Will we be together again?"

64.　You, bird, chattering parrot,
　　　Please stay quiet!
　　　Sister thrush of the willow grove
　　　Is singing us a beautiful song.

65.　The powerful dragon behind me
　　　Doesn't scare me at all
　　　When I am about to seize
　　　The sweet red apple before me.

66.　First, it is better not to see,
　　　So you will not fall in love;
　　　Second, it is better not to get too close,
　　　So there will be no reason for sadness later.

The traditional set of poems ended here.

67. The place we said three words of love,
    Was deep in a grove of willows;
    Except for the little thrush,
    Who else would know?

68. After the flower bloomed, it withered;
    After love became familiar, it faded.
    This season, I and the little yellow bee
    Feel the same way for the same reason.

69. The withered petals of a flower,
    The faded fancy of a lover;
    Even though her face and smile still shine,
    There is no more happiness in her heart.

70.   He chose that willow tree
From a hundred in the grove;
Even now, he doesn't know
That, inside, its heart is rotten.

71.   The high meadow has changed its color,
The leaves all fall from the trees;
The cuckoo flies home to Mön;
If a swallow is there, she will be pleased.

72.   Girls with beautiful bodies,
Tea and beer, a joy for all my senses;
Even if I died and become a god,
I could never be this happy.

73. We did nothing, but there is angry gossip
    About the little black crow and me;
    No matter what he does, there is no gossip
    About that falcon from the north.

74. The seeds of good and evil deeds
    Are planted now in secret,
    Their fruit is impossible to keep hidden:
    Each will ripen in its own way.

75. In the land of Da, the earth is warm.
    In Da, the women are beyond compare.
    If there were no impermanence or death,
    I would stay with them as long as I pleased.

76   No matter how deep the river,
     You can catch a fish with an iron hook.
     My sweetheart's bright face hides darkness within,
     So close, yet out of reach.

77. The bee was born too early.
     The flower bloomed too late.
     Such unlucky sweethearts!
     Their meeting will have to wait.

78. If changing into a russet-colored robe
     Would make anyone a lama,
     Then that golden goose above the lake
     Could guide us to nirvana.

79.   In a far land, in a distant country,
Your kind parents cannot help you.
Even so, no reason to be sad:
Someone is even kinder than your mother.
This lover who is kinder than your mother?
Cross the next pass to find her.

80.   My love is like
A walnut flower:
Hard to see by day,
Hard to get by night.

81.   Her winking eye the archer,
Her loving thought the arrow;
The upland meadow of the young man's heart
Feels sharp pain as her arrow hits its mark.

82. The eighth month comes,
    And all the world is yellow.
    Even if you glued the leaves back on the poplars,
    Autumn would still follow.

83. Delicious tea from India,
    Finer than all the others;
    I am looking at my lover,
    More beautiful I've never seen.

84. My lover, out of love with me,
    Lies still like a statue of a goddess.
    This is like buying a famous horse,
    Then finding it lame!

85.   If it's a walnut, crack it open!
        If it's a peach, chew it up!
        This year's new green apples,
        How sharp and tart they were!

86.   I've only known this girl for one day,
        Shall we spend the night together?
        In the morning, after we say goodbye,
        Plenty of time then to be alone.

87.   Tonight, I am so badly drunk,
        I'll sleep on the barmaid's shoulder.
        Tomorrow morning, when it's time to go,
        The rooster will let me know.

88.   Just come from Gong,
          You talking parrot?
          Tell me about my lover,
          Is she well down there?

89.   The thirst of a desert parched by drought
          Will not be slaked by a gentle rain.
          The thirst of this girl's desire
          Is impossible to satisfy.

90.   Around the petals of a single flower,
          Bees are buzzing.
          Around one warm-skinned woman,
          Her suitors crowd.

91.   The meadow turned all yellow,
      So the bees have left the meadow.
      A man grew old,
      So his lover left him, too.

92.   When people say this about me,
      It is no mistake:
      I have more lovers than there are
      Bees buzzing above this lake.

93.   In the warm land of Mön,
      The girls have pure white thighs.
      When their strong passions rise,
      Mön boys carry them away.

94.   All the channels of a river
          Can be dammed up into one pool.
          If your feelings are all blocked up inside,
          Then let the dam be broken!

95.   This river, like a cold stream in winter,
          Revives the rocky canyons.
          This beer, like an alcoholic nectar,
          Refreshes my tired body.

96.   Where my lover comes from or where she stays
          Is my business and no one else's.
          People may point their fingers at us,
          But I don't need approval for what I do.

97.   The waterwheel turns till the river runs dry,
Grinding the good barley and the bad.
That woman ages, year after year,
Looking for good men or for bad.

98.   Beer, one beer, two beers,
Drinking them one after another.
To make my head start spinning,
It will take more beers than these.

99.   When young, we form our habits,
As a youth, I grew fond of beer.
When I die, dry out my bones,
And grind them up for yeast to brew more beer.

100. Too soon, the stallion bolted;
    Too late, I pulled the reins.
    My star-crossed lover
    Went off to tell my secrets.

101. Climbing, climbing up
    That mountain pass, Gökar-la,
    I found a falling stream of melted ice
    Filling a crystal pool.

102. Little fish, don't be so anxious
    That the river flows so slowly.
    If you calm those hurried thoughts,
    Your body and mind will be at rest.

103.   The cuckoo came up from Mön;
               He longed for his magic tree.
               When the tree turned to autumn colors,
               The cuckoo flew home to Mön.

104.   You, bird, blue cuckoo,
               How soon will you leave for Mön?
               I need to send three messages
               To my beautiful lover there.

105.   Don't care about mountains or valleys
               That lie to the east, between here and Gong;
               When love has hold of your heart,
               Like a stallion, you can go anywhere.

106.   If you say crops planted this year
        Will not ripen in the next,
        Then kindly grant, I pray,
        The sky's fine sprinkling rains to fall.

107.   Sensory delights, illusory riches,
        Are gathered by lust, by love and hate;
        Yet, when I fell in love with her,
        The knot of lust became untied.

108.   Over the western mountains,
        White clouds boil in the sky;
        The clouds are fragrant incense smoke,
        An offering from the girl who's won my heart.

109.   If you are worried about crossing the river,
        A compassionate ferryman can help you.
        The misery of a lover's death,
        Who could ever help you blot that out?

110.   When it comes to cultivating your mind,
        Better to be like a donkey than a horse;
        While the horse is still being saddled,
        The donkey has reached the mountain pass!

111.   The yellow lotus-bee's thoughts?
        They are impossible to know.
        The leafy willow's thoughts?
        Just wishing for the fine rains to come.

112.   O little peach tree, but six feet tall,
How you blaze with blossoms!
I ask you to promise
Your fruit will ripen when it's time.

113.   The sun moves, lighting the whole world;
At day's end, he returns across the hills.
But my lover, object of my desire,
Never came back to me across those hills.

114.   Where does the wind rise?
It rises in a far-off country.
The body of my sweet lover
Came to me on the unerring wind.

115.   If people who only repeat what they have heard,
         Can be believers in the Three Doctrines,
         Then you, bird, talking parrot,
         Should be preaching the Buddha's Law.

116.   The ferryboat's horse-head stands so tall,
         Prayer flags flowing out behind it in the wind.
         Don't worry, set your heart at ease,
         Our love was destined before we were born.

117.   As it came from the eastern mountains,
         I imagined it a beautiful deer.
         But, when it reached the western slopes,
         I only saw a crippled antelope.

118.   Beneath her flashing eyes,
        Flows down a gentle rain of tears.
        My lover, your kind heart
        And modesty are plain for all to see.

119.   A white grouse on far-off mountain,
        A little thrush on nearby hill:
        My life's karma now exhausted,
        Alone, I can't love either one.

120.   Outside, ringed by iron mountains,
        Inside dwells a jewel.
        Jewels like sunstones and moonstones
        Are jewels from far-off India.
        The jewel that protects our land Tibet,
        Lives among us, in the Potala.

Notes to the Poems

1.   Here and in poem #35, "a young girl" (Tibetan *ma skyes a ma*), is literally "not born a mother." Theories abound to explain the unusual Tibetan turn of phrase. In a religious interpretation, it might be a reference to his own mother, or perhaps to a figurative spiritual "unborn mother" among many, even more esoteric possibilities. In the folk tradition, it is merely a reference to his current lover.

9.   The goose is a symbol of fidelity. Like the faithful goose, he, too, stayed with his lover until her rejection became too much to bear.

10.   Large ferryboats sometimes had carved horse heads at the bow, turned as if to look back into the boat. Another word for ferryboat is "dagochen" (Tibetan *rta mgo can*), literally "having a horse's head."

20.   "Ginseng" refers to *Codonopsis pilosula* (Tibetan *klu bdud rdo rje*). Codonopsis is a climbing flowering vine with various common names in English, among them Dangshen (from Chinese *dang-shen*), Bonnet Bellflower, Poor-man's Ginseng or False Ginseng. A less expensive alternative to real ginseng (*Panax ginseng*), it is also used to enhance vital energy. "Perdition" in this case would mean rebirth in one of the lesser—non-human—realms of existence.

25.   Gong (Tibetan *kong*) is a district in southeastern Tibet.

26.   A man would sometimes give his prospective bride a turquoise to wear in her hair on their wedding day.

28.   "By chance" is literally "like a bird finds a stone in the road" (Tibetan *bya rdo lam phrad*), something very random. The "bad karma" he refers to may be pregnancy, in which case in the last line he is asking the barmaid to raise the baby.

30.   This poem refers to "Prince Norsang," a popular Tibetan opera of the period, which was based on the Jataka story of Prince Sudhana and the fairy goddess Manohara. Jataka stories are tales of the Buddha's many previous rebirths. In this story, a hunter named Halaka (Tibetan *spang legs byin pa*) captures a beautiful fairy named Manohara (Tibetan *yid 'phrog lha mo*). An old hermit persuades Halaka that such a wonderful creature cannot marry a mere hunter, so he must give her to Prince Sudhana (Tibetan *nor bzang rgya lu*). Since Prince Sudhana is a reincarnation of the Buddha, the hermit persuades Halaka that the Prince is a more fitting husband for Manohara. Halaka reluctantly agrees and Manohara becomes Prince Sudhana's wife.

34.   The words "place of refuge" (Tibetan *skyabs gnas*) are a droll echo of this common Buddhist formula, comparable to a confession of faith: *sangs rgyas kyi skyabs su mchi'o / chos kyi*

skyabs su mchi'o / dge 'dun kyi skyabs su mchi'o "I take refuge in the Buddha, I take refuge in his teachings, I take refuge in the community of monks."

39.   "That man, neither lay nor monk" (Tibetan *ban de skya min ser min*) is literally, "that monk, neither white nor yellow." White denotes the laity and yellow the monkhood, so this monk is neither layman nor true monk. Some readers find here a criticism of the overbearing regent Sanggye Gyatso.

46.   Mön (Tibetan *mon*) is now part of India, located in the lowlands along the India-Tibet border east of Bhutan, in the Tawang District of Arunachal Pradesh. The Sixth Dalai Lama was born in Mön.

51.   Chongjay (Tibetan *'phyongs rgyas*) is a valley in the Yarlung region of central Tibet, southeast of Lhasa

54.   "Sagacious Ocean of Melody" (Tibetan *rig 'dzin tshangs dbyangs rgya mtsho*), is a fuller version of the Sixth Dalai Lama's name: Rigdzin Tsangyang Gyatso. Shö (Tibetan *zhol*) is the part of the old town of Lhasa located immediately below Red Hill at the bottom of the steps leading down from the Potala Palace. In Tsangyang Gyatso's day it seems to have been the pleasure quarter of the town.

57.   After the Chinese invasion and annexation of Tibet

in 1951, the eastern parts of Tibet were immediately incorporated into China, leaving the so-called Tibetan Autonomous Region considerably smaller than the original country of Tibet had been. Litang (Tibetan *li thang*, Chin. *Litang*) is now well inside the borders of Sichuan Province, about 350 kilometers west of Chengdu. The Seventh Dalai Lama was discovered there, a few years after the death of the Sixth.

73.   In "falcon from the North" (Tibetan *rgya khra hor pa*), the "North" may refer either to Mongolia or to the northeastern provinces of Tibet, now making up China's Qinghai province.

75.   "The land of Da" (Tibetan *dvags yul* or *dvags po*) is a region in south-central Tibet.

101.   The Gökar Pass (Tibetan *rgod dkar la*) is on the route from Lhasa to Samye.

117.   From a distance, he thought a woman looked beautiful, but when she came closer he realized he had been mistaken.

Bibliography

The Poems: Editions

Rig 'dzin tshangs dbyangs rgya mtsho'i gsung mgur dang gsang ba'i rnam thar. [The Secret Biography and Poems of Rigdzin Tsangyang Gyatso.] Beijing: Renmin chubanshe, 1981.

Tshangs dbyangs rgya mtsho. *Rgyal ba tshangs dbyangs rgya mtsho'i mgul glu.* [The Dalai Lama Tsangyang Gyatso's Poems.] Varanasi: Kalsang Lhundup Buddhist Temple, n.d.

Tshangs dbyangs rgya mtsho. *Tshangs dbyangs rgya mtsho'i mgul glu.* [Tsangyang Gyatso's Poems.] N.p., n.d.

Tshangs dbyangs rgya mtsho. *Tshangs dbyangs rgya mtsho'i mgul glu snyan 'grugs kyis bkod pa.* [Tsangyang Gyatso's Poetry Arranged into Individual Poems.] Appendix IX to Das, Sarat Chandra. *An Introduction to the Grammar of the Tibetan Language.* Darjeeling, 1915.

The Poems: English Translations

Love Songs of the Sixth Dalai Lama. Yu Dawchyuan [Yu Daoquan], trans. Academia Sinica, Monographs, series A, vol. 5. Beijing: Academia Sinica, 1930.

Sørenson, Per K. *Divinity Secularized: an Inquiry into the Nature and Form of the Songs Ascribed to the Sixth Dalai Lama.* Wiener Studien zur Tibetologie und Buddhismuskunde, vol. 25. Vienna: Arbeitskreis für Tibetische und Buddhistische Studien Universität Wien, 1990.

Songs of Love, Poems of Sadness: The Erotic Verse of the 6th Dalai Lama. Paul Williams, trans. London: IB Taurus, 2004.

Stallion on a Frozen Lake: Love Songs of the Sixth Dalai Lama. Coleman Barks, trans. Athens, Georgia: Maypop Books, 1993.

The Turquoise Bee: the Love Songs of the Sixth Dalai Lama. Rick Fields and Brian Cutillo, trans. San Francisco: Harper Collins, 1994.

Wings of the White Crane: Poems of Tshangs dbyangs rgya mtsho (1683-1706). Gary W. Houston, trans. Historical Introduction by Helmut Hoffmann. Delhi: Motilal Banarsidass, 1982.

GENERAL REFERENCE

Batchelor, Stephen. *The Tibet Guide.* London: Wisdom Publications, 1987.

Chan, Victor. *Tibet Handbook: a Pilgrimage Guide.* Emeryville, CA: Avalon Travel Publishing, 1994.

Dowman, Keith. *The Power-Places of Central Tibet: The Pilgrim's Guide.* New York: Routledge & Kegan Paul, 1988.

Govinda, Lama Anagarika. *Foundations of Tibetan Mysticism.* New York: Samuel Weiser, 1969.

Hoffmann, Helmut. *The Religions of Tibet.* London: George Allen & Unwin, 1961.

Hu, Shui-ying. *An Enumeration of Chinese Materia Medica.* Hong Kong: The Chinese University Press, 1980.

Lha sa'i spro skyid lta skor gyi sa khra. [Sightseeing Map of Lhasa.] Beijing: Renmin chubanshe, 1980.

Lo Hsiang-lin, compiler. *Materials Pertaining to Tibet in the Veritable Records of the Ming and Ch'ing Dynasties.* Hong Kong: Centre of Asian Studies, University of Hong Kong, 1981.

Snellgrove, David and Hugh Richardson. *A Cultural History of Tibet.* New York: Frederick A. Praeger, 1968.

The Mountains of Central Asia. Compiled by the Royal Geographical Society and the Mount Everest Foundation. London: Macmillan, 1987.

Tong Jinhua. *Zangzu Gudian Wenxue.* [Tibetan Classical Literature.] Changchun: Jilin jiaoyu chubanshe, 1989.

Tshang dbyangs rgya mtsho'i gsang rnam. [The Secret Biography of Tsangyang Gyatso.] Lhasa: Xizang renmin chubanshe, 1981.

Tucci, Giuseppe. *Tibet.* München: Nagel Verlag, 1973.

Zhongguo Lishi Dituji. [An Historical Atlas of China.] Shanghai: Ditu chubanshe, 1982. 9 vols.

Zhonghua Renmin Gongheguo Dituji Diming Suoyin. [An Index to Place Names in the "Atlas of the Peoples Republic of China."] Beijing: Ditu chubanshe, 1983.

Zhonghua Renmin Gongheguo Dituji. [Atlas of the Peoples Republic of China.] Beijing: Ditu chubanshe, 1984.

Finding List

Per Sørenson's book is a careful translation and explication of the first sixty-six poems. He also includes, in an appendix, the transliterated text of a much larger set transcribed from a Tibetan manuscript he saw in Peking. Where my selection corresponds with poems from his appendix, the numbers are enclosed in square brackets. Williams translates Sorenson's #1-66 in the same order. Note that a few of Barks' versions are difficult to identify in the Tibetan originals. He also translates one poem (#49) differently on two different pages. Fields combined #53 and #54, rearranging the couplets. Dhondup and Houston used the same source text, but Houston chose a different way of dividing poems #50-56. Those are indicated by using lower-case letters to represent the order of the lines. All references are to the numbered sequence of the poems in each book, except for Barks, where they represent page numbers.

#	Sorenson	Dhoundup	Houston	Fields	Barks
1	1	1	1	1	43
2	2	2	2	39	42
3	3	3	3	8	41
4	4	4	4	9	40
5	5	5	5	7	39
6	6	6	6	44	38
7	7	7	7	33	34
8	8	8	8	40	33
9	9	9	9	41	32
10	10	10	10	26	14
11	11	-	-	34	-
12	12	12	11	14	15
13	13	12	12	29	16
14	14	13	13	47	17
15	15	14	14	6	18

#	Sorenson	Dhoundup	Houston	Fields	Barks
16	16	15	15	58	19
17	17	16	16	59	20
18	18	17	17	60	21
19	19	18	18	56	22
20	20	19	19	62	70
21	21	20	20	5	44
22	22	21	21	10	45
23	23	22	22	15	46
24	24	23	23	57	47
25	25	-	-	3	-
26	26	-	-	17	-
27	27	24	24	18	48
28	28	-	-	35	-
29	29	-	-	46	-
30	30	25	25	27	49
31	31	26	26	28	50
32	32	27	27	24	51
33	33	28	28	25	52
34	34	29	29	42	53
35	35	30	30	20	54
36	36	31	31	23	37
37	37	32	32	32	13
38	38	33	33	52	36
39	39	34	34	38	63
40	40	35	35	45	23
41	41	36	36	30	35
42	42	37	37	16	55
43	43	38	38	31	56
44	44	39	39	19	57
45	45	40	40	61	58
46	46	41	41	11	59
47	47	-	-	43	-
48	48	42	42	22	60
49	49	43	43	13	12&72
50	50	44	44abcd/ 45ab	49	61

#	Sorenson	Dhoundup	Houston	Fields	Barks
51	51	45	45cd 46ab	4	24
52	52	46	46cd 47ab	54	25
53	53	47	47cd 49ab	55abgh	61
54	54	48	48	55cdef	-
55	55	49	49cd 50ab	21	64
56	56	50	50cd 51abcd	64	27
57	57	51	52	67	66
58	58	52	53	66	28
59	59	-	-	12	65
60	60	-	-	2	67
61	61	-	-	51	29
62	62	-	-	50	68
63	63	-	-	-	30
64	64	-	-	48	62
65	65	-	-	37	69
66	66	-	-	36	31
67	[24]	-	-	-	-
68	[30]	-	-	-	-
69	[32]	-	-	-	-
70	[340]	-	-	-	-
71	386]	-	-	-	-
72	[42]	-	-	-	-
73	[53]	-	-	-	-
74	[86]	-	-	-	-
75	[87]	-	-	-	-
76	[71]	-	-	-	-
77	[110]	-	-	-	-
78	[116]	-	-	-	-
79	[127]	-	-	-	-
80	[382]	-	-	-	-
81	[220]	-	-	-	-

#	Sorenson	Dhoundup	Houston	Fields	Barks
82	[221]	-	-	-	-
83	[369]	-	-	-	-
84	[57]	-	-	-	-
85	[171]	-	-	-	-
86	[26]	-	-	-	-
87	[36]	-	-	-	-
88	[410]	-	-	-	-
89	[55]	-	-	-	-
90	[77]	-	-	-	-
91	[111]	-	-	-	-
92	[450]	-	-	-	-
93	[121]	-	-	-	-
94	[239]	-	-	-	-
95	[230]	-	-	-	-
96	[252]	-	-	-	-
97	[78]	-	-	-	-
98	[351]	-	-	-	-
99	[283]	-	-	-	-
100	[312]	-	-	-	-
101	[322]	-	-	-	-
102	[349]	-	-	-	-
103	[396]	-	-	-	-
104	[421]	-	-	-	-
105	[424]	-	-	-	-
106	[439]	-	-	-	-
107	[49]	-	-	-	-
108	[89]	-	-	-	-
109	[131]	-	-	-	-
110	[176]	-	-	-	-
111	[179]	-	-	-	-
112	[207]	-	-	-	-
113	[277]	-	-	-	-
114	[90]	-	-	-	-
115	[117]	-	-	-	-
116	[231]	-	-	-	-
117	[236]	-	-	-	-

#	Sorenson	Dhoundup	Houston	Fields	Barks
118	[413cd/ 414ab]	-	-	-	-
119	[313]	-	-	-	-
120	[229]	-	-	-	-

THE TRANSLATOR

Geoffrey R. Waters earned a B.A. in History and Chinese from Vanderbilt University. After military service as a Field Artillery officer, he earned an M.B.A. in Finance and a Ph.D. in Classical Chinese, with a minor in Tibetan and Inner Asian Studies, from Indiana University. His translations have appeared in a variety of literary magazines and anthologies. He is the author of *Three Elegies of Ch'u: an Introduction to the Traditional Interpretation of the Ch'u Tz'u*, University of Wisconsin Press, 1985. He is currently at work on a new translation of the classic anthology *Three Hundred Tang Poems*, as well as a complete translation of the poetry of the Tang poet Du Fu. Waters is a senior credit officer at a large California bank. He and his wife live in Los Angeles, near their two grown sons.

Companions for the Journey Series

Inspirational work by well-known writers in a small-book format designed to be carried along on your journey through life.